# Dedication

To my dear wife Grace for her support and resilience during a very traumatic experience

# Acknowledgements

For use of photographs of Leatherslade farm and dairy unit
Daily Telegraph
Daily Express
Daily Herald
Daily Mail

# The Spade

To Sam
Best Wishes
John Maris
3rd March 2018

By

**John Maris**

Shield Crest

© Copyright 2017 John Maris

All rights reserved

ISBN: 978-1-911090-65-6

MMXVII

A CIP catalogue record for this book is available from the British Library

Published by
ShieldCrest Publishing Ltd.,
Aylesbury, Buckinghamshire,
HP22 5RR England
Tel: +44 (0) 333 8000 890
www.shieldcrest.co.uk

# Contents

# PROLOGUE

It was dubbed the "Crime of the century" and many people who became innocently involved had their lives permanently changed by their connection with The Great Train Robbery.

I, John Maris was one such person. I was born in Leyton, London in 1929, moved with my family to Buckinghamshire in 1940 to escape the German bombing.

I became interested in farming, helping during my holidays on the nearby farm. This was surprising as the only knowledge I had as a boy was that milk appeared on the doorstep in a bottle and potatoes and other vegetables were on my father's greengrocery stall. (It was later in life that I discovered that some of my ancestors were prominent farmers in Cambridgeshire).

I gained a scholarship to a grammar school, went to an agricultural college and began a career in agriculture.

I married Grace and we had two children, a son and daughter. In 1963 I was a herdsman working on a farm at Oakley in Buckinghamshire. My ambition was to be able to rent a farm and be a farmer in my own right.

We were happy and contented and proceeded through life without too many problems

By doing a simple and at the time insignificant act of civic duty my life and that of my family became totally transformed. The all-consuming saga of the Great Train Robbery changed all plans and ambitions.

No matter what our future roles in life would be, our destiny was to be known as "The herdsman and his family who were involved in the aftermath of The Great Train Robbery,"

# CHAPTER ONE

## Train Robbers' Hideout Discovered

It is not in very good condition now, that "T" handled ex-army trench spade. The handle is worm eaten and the metal is rusty and as I clean out the garden shed I consider, thinking that I really ought to throw it away, but then it always brings back memories, some pleasant, others not so pleasant. You see, that ex-army world war two type trench spade was used at Leatherslade Farm in Buckinghamshire, where the Great Train Robbers had their hideout. I found it there after the police had finished their detailed scene examination and left the Farm in August 1963. The spade had been used to dig a hole in which the robbers had planned to bury the evidence of their visit.

I, John Maris, was the herdsman who had notified the police of the location of the hideout. Working nearby, I looked around after the police had left and was quite surprised to find the spade standing in a small open shed in the overgrown garden. I was unaware then of the magnitude of what was to follow and how the lives of my family and myself were to be affected by this discovery.

I was a happily married man aged thirty four, with a son at grammar school and a daughter at high school. My wife Grace and I were both hardworking and contented. I had been to Agricultural College and had a fairly good job as a herdsman working for Mr Monteith at Little London Farm, Oakley. I had hopes of one day renting a farm and we were working towards that end. We lived in a modern house with all 'mod cons' and were fortunate to be progressing through life without too many complications.

On Friday July 26th 1963, I began my annual holiday and having an Austin A35 van with seats fitted at the back we were able to travel around quite easily. We spent a few days travelling locally and then on Wednesday July 31st we went to Folkestone and Dover for a couple of days camping. We travelled back on Friday August 2nd and did some shopping in Thame before driving home to Oakley. On Saturday 3rd August we went to Thame again and it was on one of these journeys home as we passed the dairy where I worked that I noticed something which at the time meant nothing but later was to prove very important. It was significant in the Great Train Robbery trial which was to follow.

Leatherslade Farm was situated on a hill secluded by trees about a quarter of a mile along a track which runs beside the dairy unit at the side of the road from Thame to Oakley. As we passed by I noticed an army type camouflaged lorry proceeding up the track towards Leatherslade Farm. I knew that the previous owners, Mr and Mrs Rixon, had moved out and that the farm had been sold. Little did I know who had purchased the farm!

John Maris and his wife Grace in the field beside the dairy unit.
Leatherslade farm is behind the trees in the far background

I began work milking on the Sunday afternoon, the following Monday was a Bank Holiday so work was reduced to milking morning and afternoon.

**John at the Dairy Farm**

On Tuesday 6<sup>th</sup> August it was back to normal working hours and I was busy all day, cleaning the milking machines and working around the dairy buildings.

Mr Monteith and Brian, the other worker, were both busy clearing the muck from the yards and transporting it to clamps in the fields. As I was working at the dairy I noticed a mini car going through the yard and on up the track towards Leatherslade Farm but did not take too much notice as I understood that there were to be new neighbours and that some alterations to the premises were to be made.

On Wednesday 7<sup>th</sup> August we were busy around the yard, when a Land Rover with some men in the back went up to the farm. They were meticulous about opening and closing the yard gates which seemed unusual during the day between milking times. We took them to be building workers for the new owners so we carried on with our work routine.

On Thursday 8<sup>th</sup> August I went milking early in the morning as usual and, after checking that the down-calving heifers in the field adjoining Leatherslade Farm were safe and well, I returned home for breakfast. (For the benefit of people who are not familiar with farming terminology, a down-calving heifer is a young cow which is heavily pregnant with its first calf. It is advisable to inspect them regularly and often to ensure that there are no complications.) By the time I returned to the dairy at 9.15 or so, Brian was already working in the yards.

About 10 o'clock Mr Monteith came to help and mentioned that the news on the radio was that there had been a train robbery at Cheddington. Our first reaction was "Who would want to pinch a train?" Mr Monteith explained that the robbers had attacked the mail train, uncoupled the front carriages and escaped with a large sum of money. The police were looking for the robbers and had asked for the public's assistance. For some strange reason, which to this day I cannot fathom, I made the facetious remark "Well, they will be up at Leatherslade Farm." At that very time our movements around the farm and buildings were being watched by a lookout posted in a tree at the entrance to Leatherslade Farm. Later the police found a large number of cigarette ends beneath that tree!

A shared smile and a shrug, and we proceeded with our work carting manure to the fields.

Friday was a routine working day: there was some discussion about the newspaper and radio reports about the train robbery, which had happened about twenty five miles away. Brian later remembered seeing a man pushing a bicycle along the road with a suitcase resting on the handlebars, but nothing else untoward.

Saturday 9th August I worked the normal Saturday routine, milking in the morning, going home to breakfast, then returning to wash the dairy equipment, the parlour, and the yards before going home again about 11 am.

I returned in the afternoon, arriving at the dairy at approximately 3.15 to collect the cows from the field adjoining the track and begin milking. I would finish about 5 pm.

At this point I think it appropriate to mention that the two gates which crossed the track leading to Leatherslade Farm would have been closed whilst milking was in progress: this forms the dispersal yard for the cows after they have been milked. Any traffic going in or out of Leatherslade Farm would have to stop and someone would have to open those gates. Whether I was in the parlour adjoining that yard or fetching cows into the parlour, I could see the track towards Leatherslade Farm. There was no movement or traffic on that track that afternoon.

Sunday was my day off. Mr Monteith did the milking that day. I used the day to view two county council smallholdings which were soon to become available as tenancies. I had been on the waiting list for many years. At approximately 6 pm I took my family to Waterperry to visit my wife's parents. As we travelled along the road between Oakley and Worminghall I saw a helicopter which landed in a field next to the road. Approaching the entrance to the field, a car came out at high speed and went quickly towards Worminghall. Nothing unusual perhaps except that it made me more aware because of the speed it went in front of me! On our return journey there was a shower of rain, which was not significant then but which was to prove important in my evidence at the subsequent trial.

On Monday 12$^{th}$ August I completed the milking in the morning as usual and went home to breakfast. The newspapers were full of the story of the train robbery and the scale of the robbery had escalated, the sum of money stolen now reported as in the region of £2,600,000.

This was the biggest robbery ever and the way in which it had been carried out demonstrated that it had been planned in great detail and that those involved were quite ruthless as was evident from the attack on the train driver, Mr Jack Mills. The police were now reported to be looking for a hideout within a thirty mile radius of Cheddington.

When I returned to the dairy at about 9 am my first job was to inspect the down-calving heifers in the field adjacent to Leatherslade Farm. It so happened that particular morning that the heifers were in close proximity to the hedge and spinney between the two Farms. After inspecting the heifers I decided to take a closer look at the farmhouse and climbed through a gap in the hedge. As I arrived on the right of way track which passes between the farmhouse and the outbuildings, I was immediately struck by the unusual scene in front of me. The windows of the house had been draped with various covers as curtains but it was odd because they were drawn fully across the windows with only the bottom corners in the centre drawn back. I became a little nervous, having read the papers that morning and being aware of the scale of the robbery and the ruthlessness of those people involved. Despite my trepidation, I continued to examine my surroundings. As I walked past the house I noticed a rope coiled up outside the back door. There were new padlocks on the garage doors and a Land Rover inside the garage in camouflage colours. There was a lorry which had been painted yellow parked under a shed with a tarpaulin covering it except for the bonnet. I did not hang about as I was not sure if anyone was in occupation and I was not going to try and find out!

Why would anyone in an isolated house on top of a hill want to black out the windows in that way? I knew then that this was the hideout of the train robbers that the police were looking for. I made my way down the track to the dairy and noticed on the way that there were no new vehicle tracks out of the farm since the rain on the Sunday evening. I could tell because although it was a hard stone track, when it rained silt tended to form in the hollows by the gates.

I went straight back to my home and reported my suspicions to my wife and to Mr Monteith. I used his telephone to inform the police at Aylesbury on the hotline which had been organized for information. I told the sergeant at the police station what I had seen, that I was sure that this was the hideout, and gave him the location.

Mr Monteith was due to go on holiday that day and I was left responsible for the day to day running of his farm. I didn't know then how difficult that was to become.

I went back to the dairy and began my main weekly wash routine which consisted of dismantling and thoroughly washing and sterilising all the milking equipment. This would entail that I would be at the dairy for the whole morning. I fully expected the police to arrive and go to Leatherslade Farm. During the afternoon I carried on with my work but paid particular attention to Leatherslade Farm to see if there was any activity—nothing happened.

After tea I decided to inspect some other cattle further afield. I took my wife, Grace, with me in our van and went past the dairy unit towards Thame, parking in the gateway of a field which rose up a hill overlooking Leatherslade Farmhouse. There were some younger cattle in that field and I thought that whilst I was checking them I would see if anything was happening at the Farm. I knew that there was no mains electricity there, but there was a generator to supply lighting and power. I wanted to find out if that engine was running. I heard nothing from the Farm, but what *was* interesting was that as we were walking across the field a car went by towards Thame and the driver sounded his horn three times. I suspect that the person in the car saw us walking in that direction and wanted to warn whoever was at Leatherslade Farm.

The police did not arrive on the Monday. On Tuesday I milked in the morning as usual and went home to breakfast, and decided that I had better ring the police again. I did so about 8 am and spoke to the same officer as on the Monday who recalled our conversation. I told him that I was convinced that Leatherslade Farm was the hideout of the train robbers and was worthy of serious investigation.

I carried on with my work at the dairy unit and was in the process of moving some cattle when at about 11 am two police officers arrived on motorcycles, one a Sergeant the other a Constable from the local Police Station at Brill. In a very casual manner they said they had received a report to investigate a farmhouse. I told them that I had reported my suspicions and they then asked where Leatherslade Farm was. I told them it was along the track and advised them to approach with care as I was not sure if anyone was there. I was surprised that these officers did not know where Leatherslade Farm was situated as it was clearly named on the Ordnance Survey Map, and was within the parish of Brill. About half an hour later the Constable came down the track to tell me that I had really started something. How true his words proved to be! These officers had obviously entered the farmhouse and discovered that my suspicions were correct.

14  Daily Telegraph and Morning Post, Wednesday, August 14, 1963

*Police swoop on isolated Leatherslade Farm*

# Hide-out of Great Train Robbery gang

It was not until around 2 pm that a large contingent of police and detectives arrived, closely followed by an onslaught of the press and the media. I could never have imagined to what extent journalists and the public could besiege a place. That afternoon it became almost impossible to carry on with my work. There were helicopters and aeroplanes circling to take photographs, police searching the fields and hedgerows, and press and media reporters talking to anybody and everybody who was around.

Once the news had spread to the villagers of Oakley there were all sorts of stories of seeing robbers fleeing across the fields with the police chasing them. It became very hectic.

NEWLY DUG PIT

LAND-ROVER USED BY GANG

WINDOWS CURTAINED

The lair—where the gang told neighbours of plans to build a swim pool. When police arrived, only empty mailbags were left

The police eventually sealed off the whole of Leatherslade Farm, the track leading up to it, and the dairy unit where I worked. I became a virtual prisoner in the dairy as any movement that I made was immediately photographed and if I ventured outside I was asked to give interviews to the press. That evening at home was very difficult. The police had informed the press and media that I had told them where the hideout was and from that point on our home was, effectively, blockaded. I told the journalists what I had seen at Leatherslade Farm, and photographs were taken of my family and me. It may have appeared to others that I was enjoying the glamour and notoriety but oh dear, the pressure my wife and family had to withstand at that time was overwhelming. What had I done? What had I got into? This was a totally different world to the one that I knew.

I had to carry on with my work as Mr Monteith was away and the cows had to be milked. I tried as best I could to work on Wednesday 14th but it was very difficult. I had to go to Brill Police Station in the afternoon to make a statement detailing all that I had seen and heard at the dairy and Leatherslade Farm. I was questioned by Superintendents Malcolm Fewtrell and Gerald Macarthur who were in charge of the investigations at that time.

# CHAPTER TWO

## The Press

On Wednesday 14<sup>th</sup> August the newspapers and media were full of what was happening at Leatherslade Farm and its surroundings. My photograph was prominent on the front page of most newspapers. I remember that I received messages from relatives who were obviously surprised and worried for my safety. I would never have realised, if I had not experienced it then, the tremendous pressure that reporters put on people in pursuit of a story. It was very enlightening to find out which newspapers reported truthfully and those that were more sensational and were not too particular about fabricating a story. I remember, on that Wednesday when my home was besieged by reporters and cameramen, I was amazed to see a photographer's camera thrown out of the window by a competitor. Our house and garden became open to all and sundry. It was impossible to keep them out.

The reward for information leading to arrest, conviction and recovery of the stolen money from the Great Train Robbery, as it was now called, was reported to be in the region of £260,000. The reporters naturally suggested that I would be in line for some of that money. They wanted to know what we would do with a large sum of money. Grace and I tried to dissuade them from that type of speculation and were only interested in seeing our way through the immediate future. This did not satisfy some of the press and there were wild stories of how we would spend a fortune. There was one report that my son wanted a sailing yacht and my daughter wanted a Paris gown. My son was twelve and my daughter eleven years old at that time: they had no wild dreams!

I think that the reporters from the national and international press were disappointed to find out that my family and I, as a herdsman, were not yokels living in a broken down cottage, the stereotype that they were expecting. They were grasping at a story of a poor farm worker who had hit the headlines and who would become rich beyond all his dreams. This was emphasised by two reporters from the Daily Express when they came to my house. The gentleman reporter went off to Leatherslade Farm to get his story while the lady reporter, Rita Marshal, stayed at our house–presumably to wait for her colleague. However, it appeared that she was very interested in our house and our standard of living because the next day in the Daily Express was a detailed description of our modern house with all the modern facilities. This report in the Daily Express seemed to have a different perspective on 'country life', at odds with that which the "town" reporters had up to that time. They found out that country people were not still living in the nineteenth century! This fact did not stop the cartoonists from having a field day at the expense of country folk. I have a copy of my favourite cartoon by Gilbert Wilkinson which shows a man dressed in a peasant smock outfit with his wife beside him outside a broken down cottage with chickens running freely around. The postman has just been and the man opens a letter which reads "Sir, your share of the £260,000 reward for information about the Great Train Robbery has been assessed at 15 shillings. A postal order is enclosed. Yours-------". I found that very amusing and it also made me aware of what might really happen.

The newspapers were full of pictures of Leatherslade Farm and the track leading up to it from the dairy unit. One of the aerial photographs became useful at the subsequent trial.

For many days the press and television news media people were around the farm and my house and we built up a certain rapport, but I was always conscious of the fact that I had to be careful of what I said to them. Any careless or flippant remark would soon have been headline news.

It was not long before I began to get letters from all sorts of people and from a wide variety of places. The story had spread world-wide and there were people who were quite happy to give advice as to where the money was hidden. Some of the letters were congratulatory but many were from "cranks" with all kinds of weird messages. Alas, I also received threatening letters. I suppose this was inevitable as by now the police were issuing the names of people they wished to see as a result of the clues found at Leatherslade Farm. Some of these threatening letters were bogus but others were obviously not. I remember one in particular which threatened my family and myself and which could only have been written by someone who had been at Leatherslade Farm. The letter was signed "Diana". One of the bedrooms at the farmhouse had a notice on the door which read "Diana's room"! It was not until a few years later that Grace told me that one of the letters which she had opened had a drawing of a coffin on which was written John Maris. This obviously caused her great distress.

It became clear that I had become involved with something very big and very dangerous. The hue and cry was on to find the robbers and it appeared that I was a marked man. I began to take such precautions as were possible. I realised that when the police had finished their investigations at the Farm I would be alone working at that isolated dairy unit. Grace sewed a long pocket in my trouser leg into which I placed a wooden truncheon to carry around with me. I put some hypochlorite fluid into small jars and, together with some wooden staves, I placed them at strategic places around the buildings. Thankfully I did not need to use them.

Grace and the children bought an Alsatian puppy which soon grew and became very protective. This may appear somewhat dramatic but at the time these precautions seemed very necessary. I also realised that my evidence of finding the hideout and the various movements of people whom I had seen might be crucial in a trial. I thought it prudent to engage a solicitor to advise and protect my interests. I engaged Donald Silk who had offices in Oxford and London. On my behalf he put in a claim for any reward money which might become available. I also found it advisable to watch all comings and goings at the dairy and so I began to keep a detailed diary of events and people who either were around or who contacted me. This particular decision proved to be both critical and useful at a later date.

# CHAPTER THREE

## The Hunt Was On–The First Arrests.

On Thursday 15th August Detective Chief Superintendent Tommy Butler and Detective Chief Superintendent Peter Vibart of the Flying Squad took over the investigations as it had become apparent that members of London gangs were involved in The Great Train Robbery. This became clear from the clues which were found at Leatherslade Farm. The media were giving details and printing pictures of wanted men. Two men were arrested in Bournemouth as a result of the suspicions of a lady who had been asked to rent a garage. Some money in holdalls was found in a wood in Surrey and it appeared that some of the robbers were panicking as a result of the publicity and pressure of the police enquiries. The police had spent a considerable time "taking Leatherslade Farm apart" to find any clues which might lead to the identity of the robbers. Whilst the police were there I had a degree of protection from the media and sightseers. This enabled me to get back to a steady work routine.

When the police had finished at the Farm and they had removed the vehicles and other items of interest, they handed the Farm back to Mr Rixon, as the robbers had only placed a deposit on the Farm before moving in. Being close by and working in the vicinity of the Farm I was one of the first persons to venture there after the police had left. Whilst looking around I found an ex-army trench spade in a small open shed in the overgrown garden. This spade was a match to the one which was shown in a photograph beside a hole dug in the front garden by the robbers. Realising that the police had thoroughly searched the farm I kept the spade as a memento.

# The hole at Oakley

The hole in the ground that the police discovered at Leatherslade Farm, Oakley.

Mr Rixon decided to open Leatherslade Farm for public viewing for a small entrance fee and soon the whole area around the farm and dairy unit was besieged by sightseers. Leatherslade Farm and Oakley had certainly become the place to visit.

As a result of all the publicity which had followed The Great Train Robbery and the escape of the robbers there were various allegations of mishandling of the case and of police incompetence. I do not subscribe to any of those allegations as it is so easy to be wise after the event. One particular instance of criticism came on September 10th when the MP for Twickenham, Mr Roger Gresham Cooke, made a speech in his constituency in which he criticised the villagers of Oakley and me in particular for not blocking the entrance to Leatherslade Farm with a tractor or something else to prevent the robbers from escaping; he suggested that village men should have gone there in a kind of posse and used our citizens common law rights to arrest the robbers. Oh dear! What a hue and cry he started! He was obviously not acquainted with any of the facts or details of Leatherslade Farm and I suspect that he just wanted to get onto the publicity bandwagon. Well, he certainly did that.

The villagers were justifiably outraged that an MP should think of village people as yokels with sticks and staves who would band together and take vigilante action. Mr Gresham Cooke was challenged to debate the issue on television or in the village hall. Eventually he realised his mistake and decided not to take up the invitation. To me, this was just another indication of the false impression which townspeople and the media had of those who live and work in the countryside. Just because country people are not extrovert does not mean that they are not intelligent. On the contrary, I believe that the reticence and reserve shown by country folk is allied to a greater appreciation of the things that really matter and where one's priorities lie. I may be prejudiced even though I was born in London and lived there until I was ten years old.

The villagers of Oakley had shown a great deal of common sense and I was pleased that they had supported the action which I had taken when discovering the hideout of the Great Train Robbers.

While all this media activity was happening, we were busy getting in the harvest on the farm despite the many visitors and sightseers around the buildings.

As time went by more arrests had been made, and the charges and preliminary hearings were arranged. Before being called as a witness at the court, in company with some other people, I was asked to attend various identification parades to see if I could recognise anyone who had been at Leatherslade Farm. For whatever reason, in spite of the fact that I was in the building, I was only called to one of these parades as the legal advisors of the accused men objected to my participation. I did not understand the reasons for the objections. Surely I could only either recognise them or not, and that was what identity parades were for. I have no doubt that the legal profession has an explanation for what seemed to me to be a quirk in British justice.

# CHAPTER FOUR

## Coincidences

As autumn changed to winter, fewer people visited Leatherslade Farm. The routine on the farm where I was working had changed slightly because we began alterations to the yards and the milking equipment.

It was on Sunday 24th November 1963, while I was at home, that a white hard topped Land Rover stopped outside my house. A gentleman from Greenham Common Caravan Company had just delivered two caravans to Leatherslade Farm and asked on behalf of Mr Rixon if I would hold the keys until the people who were to move into the caravans arrived. Although I had become nervous and tried to detach from the happenings at Leatherslade Farm, after checking with Mr Rixon I agreed to do as he wished.

Five days later, on the evening of Friday 29th November when night had fallen, two men arrived with their wives and young children to collect the keys to the caravans. Nothing unusual, perhaps, except that they had come from Scotland and did not know the area. They also said that they had been looking for work and were going to work 'in the sugar beet factory nearby'. When I explained the recent history of the place where they were going to live and that the nearest sugar beet factory was at least eighty miles away, they became somewhat perturbed.

Now, I had become suspicious of anyone and anything to do with Leatherslade Farm over the past few months, and wondered if what they were saying was genuine. I began to wonder why I had got involved. However I took them at their word and gave them the keys and told them where the caravans were parked. They were obviously disturbed at what I had told them but, having travelled from Scotland and having nowhere else to go, they moved in to the caravans.

The next morning, the Saturday, whilst I was working at the dairy, I met these people from the caravans and helped them as best I could with vegetables and provisions. I felt very sorry for them and their predicament and we overcame the mutual misgivings.

It was on the following day, Sunday 1ˢᵗ December, while I was at the dairy, that one of the men from the caravans came to see me to inform me that out of a sense of curiosity they had tried the keys to one of the caravans in the lock of the back door of the farmhouse and were able to unlock the door and to go inside. They noticed that the wallpaper in one of the bedrooms was identical to that in one of the caravans. These people were now really nervous. On their behalf I telephoned the police to tell them what had been found. The police carried out an investigation and concluded that this was just a coincidence. I have no reason to disagree with that decision.

It was not long before the families moved out of the caravans and found work and accommodation in Hemel Hempstead. Subsequently the caravans were removed. I did not discover why or how these families knew of the caravans for rent.

The reason it aroused my interest was because one of the Train Robbers, James White, was found living in a caravan when he was arrested. I did hear later from one of the men who had lived in one of the Leatherslade Farm caravans. During the trial for perjury he wrote to me from Chesham offering any help he might be able to give me regarding the times when I started and finished milking.

The dairy unit and yards were due for alterations in order to modernise and make the milking more efficient. We altered the layout of the collecting and dispersal yards. This entailed putting down more concrete and moving gates to other positions. The actual milking equipment was changed and brought more up to date which shortened the time spent milking the cows. The diesel engine which was used to drive the milking machine was modified to increase power and at the same time became a little noisier. I mention this because these details were to be relevant and crucial at a later date.

# CHAPTER FIVE

## The Trial

The year of 1963, historic as far as I was concerned, passed away and as 1964 arrived I had the prospect of attending the trial of the Great Train Robbers as a witness to concern my mind and activities.

The preparations for probably the greatest trial ever began with tremendous publicity and organisation at Aylesbury. It was in January 1964 that I was summonsed as a witness for the prosecution. Though I had attended Magistrate's Courts on occasion, this was something different. There was this aura of authority in the whole building and I had never experienced the feeling of trepidation which engulfed me then. I was in yet another totally different world. My anxiety was not helped by the fact that, although I had been summonsed, I was not called to testify for about three days. I was left in a room for long hours all by myself, having to watch and wait while justice took its slow course. I can remember spending the time counting the number of bricks in each wall!

Eventually I was called to give my testimony and I must admit that when I first entered that witness box and looked around and saw Mr Justice Edmund Davies, the Judge, and a battery of QC's all dressed in their wigs and gowns, the jury and then the dock with the accused men sitting there watching me, I was very nervous. Even though I had nothing to fear I had the feeling that I was going to be in for a tough time. As I was a prosecution witness, the QC for the Crown began to question me as to who I was and what I was doing at the dairy beside the track which led to Leatherslade Farm. I gave my testimony of times that I had been working there, the vehicles that I had seen and the dates and times that I had seen them. I went through the explanation of visiting the heifers in the field beside the farm, of getting through the hedge and what I had seen there and my telephone calls to the police. Everything that I said was questioned in detail to make sure that I could not have been mistaken. I was shown various exhibits to confirm that they were what I had seen: the coil of rope, padlocks, photographs of the lorry in the shed and the Land Rover in the garage. This all seemed straightforward and some of my fears went away.

The barrage began when the QC's for the defence of the accused began their cross examination. My, how they tried to intimidate me and to throw me off balance. There were all sorts of questions about my integrity and assurance of what I had seen and had related to the court. I found it very difficult to keep my cool as I felt that I was on trial. I remember one particular question from one of the defending QC's. He asked me about my statement that I did not think that anyone had left Leatherslade Farm after the Sunday evening after the robbery as there were no vehicle tracks out by the gateway near the dairy unit. I was immediately questioned in great detail of how I could be sure of this. I explained that I was sure because it had rained on that Sunday afternoon and silt had built up in the hollows by that gate. The silt had not been disturbed by the time I had gone through that gate on the Monday morning. This was still not satisfactory for that QC. "Did you get down on your knees to examine that silt?" I am afraid that at that point I did lose my cool and icily explained how that was not necessary. I suppose that he was only doing his job.

I was very impressed with the attitude of the Judge; he was very polite and made me more at ease by the manner in which he controlled the QC's for the defendants when they appeared very aggressive. I was not sorry when that cross examination was over and I could leave. I was told to be prepared to be called back to the Court at short notice if that proved to be necessary.

I carried on with my work at the dairy and it was quite noticeable how the publicity of the trial created a new interest in Leatherslade Farm and the dairy unit itself. There were more visitors to the area and some of them were very interested in the trial and the evidence which I had given. This became obvious from the type of questions they were asking and the notice they were taking of what one could see and hear from the area where I was working. I began to keep more detailed diary notes of the people who questioned me in that way.

The trial continued and it was on Sunday February 9th 1964 at about 1.30 while I was at home with my family, having just had lunch, when we had visitors. Two men came to the door and wished to ask me some questions about the evidence which I had given in court. I was not happy at being questioned about my evidence away from the Trial Court and asked them who they were and what were the reasons for the questions. One of the men gave me a visiting card with his name on it, Mr Denman. He said that they were solicitors for the defence and wished to question me about the time I was milking the cows at the dairy on the Saturday after the train robbery. He said that the alibis of some of the accused were that they had gone to the farm after the robbery to deliver some vegetables in a lorry and then went into the farmhouse to wash their hands and that is why their fingerprints were found there. I told these men that I had given my evidence in Court and since I was still under the jurisdiction of the Court I was unable to help them.

I was not happy about this visit and wrote on the visiting card that they were solicitors for the defence, the time and date of the visit and the registration number of the car which they were driving. I also telephoned the police to inform them of the incident. A short while later, after they had made enquiries, the police told me that the visitors were not solicitors: they were private investigators who had been hired by the defence solicitors. I was told that the next day in Court the Judge reprimanded the defence counsel for this breach of the rules. I also heard from people in the village that those two men had been asking villagers about my background and integrity. They were obviously searching for any information which they could use to malign my character and make me appear an unreliable witness. They were unlucky in their search.

The trial proceeded and the defence counsel began to put the case for the accused men. Back at the farm there were certainly more visitors and I continued to keep details of times, descriptions and car numbers of those people who were unknown to me. This may seem rather dramatic, but my experiences had led me to be suspicious of everyone and anything.

So it was March 9th 1964 that I was recalled to attend the Court to be cross examined again about the evidence which I had already given, which in effect disproved the alibis of those accused who said that they had visited the farm after the robbery. The counsel for the defence really began to apply pressure. They used some legal expression to the effect that I had been in collusion with my solicitor, Mr Donald Silk, who had attended the trial daily and had heard the alibis in court. I explained that I did not know what their terminology meant and that I had not discussed the matter with Donald Silk. The Judge was very polite and helpful and explained what the defence counsel was trying to suggest. When I told them that the first I heard of the alibis was from the private investigators which they had sent to interview me they became less enthusiastic in pursuing that point.

There were questions as to what I could see from the dairy unit and when I said that I was able to see a long way up the track to Leatherslade Farm as I collected the cows into the milking parlour, the QC disputed this and said that the police drawing of the area showed that was not possible. I had to prove to this counsel that the police plan was not to scale, which the police agreed, and that there was a curve in the track which the aerial photographs showed. Not happy with my having proved him wrong, the QC then said that there was a hedge behind the dairy unit which prevented me from seeing up the track. I told him that there was no hedge behind the dairy unit as the photographs showed very clearly and that if he did not believe me then he should come to the dairy unit and see for himself. This QC said that he had been there. He was obviously trying to unnerve me. The questioning continued and I was getting very irritated that they were trying to make me appear a liar. Eventually I was allowed to leave the witness box and to return home. Two days later two men were taking photographs of the track and the buildings.

Once again the pressure on my family and I was built up by the press questions and the stress of the trial. How my wife Grace and the children withstood the constant anxiety at that time I shall never know. I shall be eternally thankful for the way in which Grace managed to withstand the pressure and to hold the family together. Even before the end of the trial the newspaper reporters began to visit us to discuss the reward money and what we would do. I tried to explain that the trial was not yet over and they were premature in their request for a story.

The trial came to a conclusion with the counsel and the Judge giving their summing up. It was March 20th 1964 when the jury were sent out to consider their verdicts. They were sent to a secret location as it was thought that they would be out for a considerable time and security was very necessary. Six days later, on March 26th, the jury returned to give their verdicts. There were many guilty verdicts for robbery and conspiracy to rob.

It was not until April 16<sup>th</sup> that the Judge gave his sentences and what a reaction they provoked! 30 year sentences had never been given before for robbery and that certainly began a debate nationwide as to the justification for such a sentence. The train robbers began their prison sentences and attention was then drawn to the details of how they were caught and proven guilty.

Detective Superintendent Fewtrell wrote a book and within it he described how the clues found at Leatherslade Farm were important in the arrest and convictions of the robbers. It would have been difficult to convict them without their known presence at the Farm.

I have read in another book that some of the robbers were on the way back to burn down the farm on the Tuesday 13<sup>th</sup> August when they heard a broadcast that the police had arrived at their hideout. They then had to change plans and go into hiding.

If I had not reported the location of the hideout to the police on the Monday morning and then rung the police again on the Tuesday morning expressing my conviction that Leatherslade Farm was the hideout which they had been looking for, I believe that the farm and outbuildings would have been burnt down and any evidence of their occupation would have been destroyed. The Great Train Robbers might then have managed to avoid capture and prosecution.

# CHAPTER SIX

## Summer 1964 – Reward and Being Under Observation

After the trial I carried on with my work and the visitors increased in number and, especially during August 1964, there were some who seemed to be paying particular attention to my movements. At various times there were cars parked by the roadside and the occupants were watching me through binoculars. I made special notes in the diary of the dates, times, car numbers and descriptions of those people who appeared to be most interested in what I was doing. The publicity which followed the trial also brought families who were interested in the dairy routine and then they would walk up the track to Leatherslade Farm. Many of these people took photographs of the dairy, the cows and the farm itself.

One such visitor was a Mr Derek Agnew who came to see me while I was working at the dairy. Mr Agnew said he was an author and was writing a book about The Great Train Robbery and requested that I give him an interview to detail my involvement in the Train Robbery Saga. I had seen him around the area two or three times before and believed that he *was* gathering material for his book. On one occasion he brought some children with him while I was milking and seemed to show great interest in the routine. I told Mr Agnew that he should contact my solicitor, and if he was agreeable, I would give him an interview. Donald Silk, my solicitor, checked out Derek Agnew's credentials and found out that he was indeed a writer.

So it was that a few weeks later Mr Agnew arrived at my house with a lady he introduced as his wife and we began discussing what I had seen and the times that I worked at the dairy before and after the robbery. Mr Agnew made notes of our conversation and my wife and children were present during our discussion. I considered that we had a friendly and sociable interview and Grace made refreshments for Derek Agnew and his wife. The conversation spread over family life, our children, and the reason for getting our Alsatian dog, during which Mr Agnew typed up his notes. Before they left I asked for and got a typed copy of what we had been discussing and the notes which he had made. I asked him when the book would appear and was told that he did not know as he had a great deal more material to gather.

The Train Robbery Saga had not ended with the sentencing: there were still some persons who the police were hunting. On August 12th 1964 Charles Wilson escaped from Winson Green prison, and so interest erupted again.

Speculation returned again to the reward money, and who was going to receive what amount. The newspapers and other media recommenced their inquisitiveness, and there were cartoons and various attempts to stir up controversy between the reward seekers. On August 24th 1964 I was asked to go to London to receive a cheque for £ 15,000 from the loss adjusters for the information that I had given to the police about the location of the train robbers' hideout. Subsequently another £3,000 arrived from other sources which had offered rewards. My solicitor arranged for Grace and myself to stay overnight at the London Hilton hotel and amid great publicity we received the cheque. We remained in London the following day to look around the shops, but we did not go on a spending spree, that was not our nature.

When we returned home we settled back into a routine knowing that we had a little more security as far as finance was concerned. I bought a new car and had decided to leave my job and buy a house.

My ambition of having a farm to rent had been thwarted when I was told by the Oxfordshire County Council Smallholdings Committee that my name would be taken off their list for the tenancy of a farm. They gave no explanation for this. I assumed that, because I had received reward money, they thought I would be able to rent a smallholding privately. At that time there were very few farms to rent and there was little prospect of tenanting a farm unless the applicant was a farmer's son and had his parents support. [Later in life I did become a farm manager on a large estate.]

As we were living in a tied cottage which went with the job, we thought that this was the opportunity to break away and to purchase a house of our own. In September 1964 we bought a new detached house in Quainton, near Aylesbury. I began work at the New Holland Machine Company in Aylesbury believing that I could put the saga of the train robbery behind me.

# CHAPTER SEVEN

## Perjury!

Grace and I had settled into our new house at Quainton and the children were quite happy at the Grammar School and the High School in Aylesbury. I had settled in to my new job and life had become pleasant and peaceful. We had decided to have a family party at a hotel in Thame, and this was arranged for an evening just before Christmas 1964.

On December 8th I returned home late from work, we had been working on overtime at the factory, and as I turned into the close in which our house was situated I was confronted by a large number of reporters and cameramen. As I got out of the car I asked what was going on. You can imagine my surprise when I was told that I had been arrested on a charge of perjury! I had great difficulty in convincing those people that I had just returned from work. When I got indoors Grace was in a terrible state of anxiety and shock. While Grace and the children, after returning from school, were watching television, there had been a news flash that John Maris had been arrested for giving perjured evidence at the Great Train Robbery trial. The effect on Grace and the children had been traumatic. They did not know what had happened and assumed that I had been arrested at work. I just could not believe it. How could such an accusation arise? How could it be delivered and broadcast in such a manner? I could only conclude that the train robbers and their supporters were out for revenge and intended to cause my family and myself as much distress as possible. Even after all the years that have passed I cannot forgive those responsible for causing us the worry and trauma visited on us that day.

I was told that I had to go round to the local police station to find out what was going on. The local policeman had instructions to take my fingerprints and I had to fill in a form for bail of £300. The police were unable to help me with any information about the charge. Even more mysterious, when I telephoned Donald Silk, my solicitor, to find out what was happening he did not know either. Apparently someone had applied for a warrant for my arrest on a charge of perjury without giving precise details, and it had been granted. How this could happen in the British system of justice is still a mystery to me. Later we found out that a warrant had been taken out at Aylesbury Magistrate's Court. This was a private prosecution brought by George Wisbey, the brother of Thomas Wisbey who had been jailed for his part in the robbery.

The charge stated in the warrant was that 'as a sworn witness on March 9th 1964 John Maris made a statement which he knew to be false or did not himself believe'. No further details were given. As my solicitor was unable to obtain any more details of what I was supposed to have done, we had to conduct our own investigation. On March 9th I had been recalled to the trial to tell of the milking routine on the Saturday *after* the robbery which in effect nullified the alibis of some of the train robbers. It now appeared that the charge against me must refer to that evidence of the milking routine, but in what way were these people claiming that I had committed perjury?

The way that this charge had been announced and the shock of finding ourselves in such a position had a devastating effect on my family. I can only say that, being a very close and loving family, we were able to withstand the pressure. Grace and the children had to overcome the trauma of seeing me on such a terrible charge. I am proud of their strength and resilience in the way the family was held together at that time. Our relatives were very supportive and understanding when I decided to cancel the family party which had been arranged.

The following weekend we visited Grace's parents at Waterperry and during the conversation Grace's mother mentioned an article which she had read in the "Oxford Times" which described a committee which had been set up to campaign against the length of the sentences which had been passed on the train robbers. We managed to find the article, and there among other members of that committee was the name of the secretary, Derek Agnew! With this information my solicitor began to investigate further the activities of Mr Agnew and it became obvious that the interview which I had granted him was not for material for a book, but to try and find a means of destroying me and the evidence which I had given in order to have the sentences of some of the robbers reviewed.

I was advised that I would require a prominent Queens Counsel to act on my behalf as defence on such a serious charge. Mr Edward Gardner QC and his deputy QC were thus engaged for my defence. I was to attend the Magistrate's Court in Aylesbury on December 22$^{nd}$ 1964 to answer the charges made against me. It was difficult to prepare any defence as the charges were so vague. All we could ascertain was that Derek Agnew was in some way involved in trying to destroy the evidence which I had given in March.

At the Magistrates Court the vague charges were read out and no further details were given. Edward Gardner QC answered the charges by explaining that the source of the perjury allegation was the vindictive malice of wicked men now acting through their relatives and was a despicable attempt to frame an innocent man, the charge being empty of merit. He asked that more specific details of the charge should be provided in order that a defence could be prepared.

Ellis Lincoln, the QC for the prosecution, asked for a stay of execution of forty eight hours so that proceedings to prevent the statement of details being handed over could be taken in the High Court. I was amazed when the magistrates agreed to this stay of execution. I was even more surprised when the prosecution were not ready to proceed with the case and the hearing was adjourned until January 28th 1965. Edward Gardner argued again at the obvious distress which such a postponement would cause, but to no avail. What is a mystery to me is that a prosecution should be able to prepare for six months to have me arrested and yet require another month to prepare a case against me. I cannot help thinking that they may have been surprised themselves that the Magistrates had agreed to their original warrant!

It was not until January 22nd 1965 that three High Court Judges decided that more details of the charges against me should be made available to my lawyers, and even then they were very vague. This gave us six days to prepare to answer the charges and we were still in the dark as to what form the prosecution was to take.

It was interesting to note the comments of the Lord Chief Justice Lord Parker at that hearing when he was reported as saying that he was puzzled as to how the Magistrates could issue an arrest warrant on the strength of the prosecution statement!

I gathered all the various notes which I had made in diaries, the copy of the transcript which Derek Agnew had made at my house and any material which I considered might be relevant to the charges against me in order to be prepared for any situation which could arise on January 28th.

January 28th 1965 was a Thursday and the day I was due to attend the Magistrate's Court in Aylesbury. Ashe Lincoln led for the prosecution and there were six charges read out. That I had lied about the time that I started milking on the Saturday after the train robbery. In the charges "it is alleged that while on oath, Maris knowingly made four false statements about the time he milked cows in sheds adjoining the track leading to Leatherslade Farm, Oakley on August 10<sup>th</sup> 1963, two days after the robbery; a false statement to the effect that he did not discuss the question of vehicles going along the track on that day with his employer; and a false statement to the effect that vehicles could not have used the track without him seeing or hearing them while he was doing the afternoon milking that day."

Ashe Lincoln QC reiterated the alibis of Robert Welch, Thomas Wisbey and James Hussey that a Ronald Dark drove Wisbey and Welch to the farm in the lorry about 3.30 on the Saturday after the robbery and that is why their fingerprints were found there, Welch's on a beer can, Wisbey's on the bath and James Hussey had left his fingerprints on the lorry before it had left London.

Thomas Wisbey and Robert Welch were brought from prison to restate those alibis. Ronald Dark, who was escorted by a warder as he was detained on an unrelated matter, also stated his part in the alibi. What surprised me was that if he drove the lorry to Leatherslade farm innocently, why were his fingerprints not found in the lorry? Did he wear gloves? If he did, why in the middle of summer? There is another flaw in the alibi given by those accused of the robbery which does not appear to have been exposed at the trial. If they drove the lorry to the farm on the Saturday afternoon as they claimed, when and why did they paint the lorry yellow at the farm and then cover it over with a tarpaulin? That the lorry had been painted at the farm was evidenced by the spillage of some paint on the floor. The spillage led to the arrest of another of the robbers when he stepped in the paint and left a clue on his shoe. I am really surprised that it was left to my evidence to break their alibi when there were other weaknesses.

The enquiry agent who had visited me on February 9<sup>th</sup> 1964 was called and said that I had told him that I was at the dairy at a different time to that which I had given in court. It was fortunate that I had kept the visiting card that he had given me. My QC, Edward Gardner, asked him for one of his visiting cards, which he produced, and then gave him the card which I had retained and on which I had written the details of his visit, that he was a solicitor for the defence at the train robbery trial, the time of his visit and the registration number of the car which he used on that day. When my QC asked him if that was his card he went quite pale as he realised that he had purported to be a solicitor. The Magistrates also realised what had happened and so his evidence was discredited. The hearing was adjourned until the next day, Friday January 29th.

The first witness to be called on the Friday was Derek Agnew. He was to give details of his visits to the dairy and to my house. I was astonished and, in fact, livid to hear him give such a warped and twisted account of what we had discussed at the interview at my house. It was very different to what had happened. He read out what he said was a copy of the transcript of that interview and it was so markedly different from the original that I had great difficulty in containing my anger. Fortunately I had my copy with me and that was read and shown to the Magistrates. When asked the whereabouts of the notes which he had made of the interview, Derek Agnew said that he had destroyed them as they were no longer necessary!

Edward Gardner QC had obviously been very busy in obtaining background material about Derek Agnew. He showed the court sleazy and pornographic magazines which Derek Agnew was involved in producing. The result of the questioning by my QC and the answers Derek Agnew gave concerning these magazines did not produce a favourable impression of his morals to the magistrates. They certainly did not on me!

Derek Agnew left the courtroom and was caught talking to another person who was yet to be called as a witness. He was then ordered by the Magistrates to remain in the courtroom and was not to lunch with Mrs De Alwiss who was the next witness to be called after the lunch break.

Mrs De Alwiss said that she had been asked by Derek Agnew to accompany him to visit my house and to pose as his wife in order that my suspicions should not be aroused. She agreed with my QC that this was an act of deceit. After cross examination she also said that after the interview at my house Derek Agnew had stopped in a lay-by and made alterations to the notes which he had made during their visit to my house. Another act of deceit. It was apparent that the people who were trying to discredit me were themselves conspirators.

Next to be called as witnesses were the so-called "Q" men. These were the enquiry agents who had been engaged by Derek Agnew to watch my movements at the dairy unit in the summer of 1964, the year after The Train Robbery. As it turned out, these were the men who I had seen in various places around the dairy and of whom I had made notes in my diary. They had been watching me and I had been observing them! These agents were called to state the times at which I was at the dairy to begin milking in the summer of 1964. Presumably, the thinking behind this was that if I started milking at three thirty in August 1963 then I would be doing the same in 1964. This showed how much the people who instigated the charges against me were ignorant of the work routine on a small mixed dairy and arable farm. Depending on harvest times and weather conditions the actual time of starting various operations is quite flexible, especially with a dairy herd that was designed to have the main calving period during the winter months. August and September were the months when there are fewer cows to milk as many are being "dried off" in order to give them a rest before they were due to calve again. Thus milking times are much more flexible during this period.

As it turned out, harvesting was late in 1963 and so I was not called upon to assist with carting corn or other jobs involved with the harvesting during that August, therefore the milking routine was not interrupted.

In 1964 harvesting was earlier and I milked the cows during a period which fitted in with helping with the harvest. Also, during the winter of 1963/1964 we had made alterations to the yards around the dairy and a different milking machine was installed. These alterations had the effect of reducing the time spent milking.

I am still amazed as to the lengths which these people went to try and discredit the evidence which I gave at the main trial. The hearing was postponed until the following Friday, February 6th 1965.

On that Friday Ellis Lincoln, for the prosecution, called my previous employer, Mr Monteith, as a prosecution witness. I was very surprised at this as Mr Monteith was a good friend as well as being my ex-employer and had been very supportive during the time of the Train Robbery Saga. I believe that Mr Monteith was also confused as to why he was being called as a witness. I also believe that he had been deceived in what role he would be called upon to play.

By some legal technicality, which I did not and still do not understand, Mr Monteith was declared a hostile witness which in effect seemed as though his being called as a prosecution witness backfired on the prosecution. Mr Monteith, in answer to my QC, Mr Edward Gardner, agreed with what I had stated, namely that the alterations to the dairy unit and the fact that harvesting was earlier in 1964 would have made the milking times irregular.

All in all the prosecution case was shown to be so bogus that Edward Gardner QC once again accused the prosecution of malevolence and vengeful motives.

I was quite surprised that it took the Magistrates one and three quarter hours to find that none of the charges against me had been made. The prosecution was still not happy and Ashe Lincoln said that he would apply to the High Court for a voluntary bill of indictment. They were still determined to make my family and I suffer. My QC asked the Magistrates to award me costs but they did not agree. That decision still sticks in my throat. Surely, I thought, if these people had brought a fraudulent prosecution against me and then lost it in such a way, I should have been entitled to reimbursement for the costs which had been incurred in clearing my name? This thought must have entered the minds of other people as I was asked if I would sue for reimbursement. At that time I was so relieved at the result that I was in no position to make a decision. Upon reflection, it was decided not to proceed, not because we thought we would not win, but because I would have been suing the relatives of the train robbers for costs incurred and it was unlikely that I would receive any money when I won the case, and still more would have to be spent in proceeding with such a prosecution.

It was not until Friday April 9th that the trauma ended when the High Court refused to issue a voluntary bill of indictment against me.

# CHAPTER EIGHT

## Reflections

My total legal costs, including the defence on the perjury charge, came to more than £4,000. That was quite a sum of money at that time, equivalent to the price of a detached house!

One day towards the end of April 1965 I had a visit from Chris Brasher, who had retired from athletics and who was then making a new career in investigative journalism. There had been media reports of the perjury trial and some people had remarked on the injustice which they felt I had received from the initial instigation of the charges against me and also the fact that I had not received an award of costs. Chris Brasher wanted to know if I would be interested in a television programme which was being prepared and which would include criticisms of the legal process which allowed injustice to happen. Although feeling bitter at the time and very tempted to appear, I had to decline the offer as I considered that I could not inflict any more anxiety upon my family by being involved in more controversy.

A few months later I was approached by some men from a firm of solicitors who were engaged in a prosecution case against Derek Agnew. I was told that he was alleged to have committed an insurance fraud in South Africa. I was asked if I would go as a witness for the prosecution to give details of the manner in which he had conspired against me. Now that was a very tempting prospect! Here was a chance to exact revenge for what he had done to me and my family. After careful consideration I decided not to go, the reason being that I had no inclination to be involved again in controversy.

One of the effects of my involvement with The Great Train robbery and subsequent events has been that my trust in people has been irrevocably damaged. Sadly, I am unable to accept people at face value. Apart from family and close friends I always look for ulterior motives when I am approached with deals or propositions. This is not a state which I like and perhaps in time I may recover my former trusting nature.

Previous to The Great Train Robbery I had a very positive attitude to British Justice. I am afraid that my experience has led me to have a rather different view. To me, it seems that the process is so elaborate and complex that it is not difficult for people with evil intent to manipulate the system in order to obtain their aims, and in the process innocent people may suffer emotionally as well as financially. I am not now surprised when I hear of people avoiding litigation even though they may have good cause to seek justice. A more cynical man might conclude that the legal system in Britain is devised in order to perpetuate a lavish income for the legal experts involved!

Upon reflection, and being wise after the event, I can see some points where I should have been more careful in the way I allowed myself to be manipulated into a position where I could be prosecuted. I think especially of the actions of Derek Agnew although at the time everything appeared to be above board and straightforward. Perhaps the biggest failing was the fact that, in an initial statement to the police after the robbery, I failed to mention that I had seen the ex-army lorry going up the track to Leatherslade Farm before the robbery took place. I had believed that it belonged to the local wood and coal man who used such vehicles and had often gone to the farm when the previous owner Mr Rixon lived there. I did not connect that army camouflaged lorry with the one which was painted yellow and left under a tarpaulin by the train robbers until it was too late. It would have appeared too convenient to mention this later when the accused had given their alibis. I could have saved myself a great deal of trouble had this vital piece of information been available to the crown prosecution. On the other hand, perhaps the accused would have been able to devise a different alibi which could not have been disputed.

The suggestion has been made that I should not have got involved in the first place and could have saved my family and myself a lot of trauma. I am afraid that argument is not a valid one for me. When the investigations by the police into the Great Train Robbery began, my information, which led the police to the hideout, was given as a responsible person in society. I am as I am and my nature would not have allowed me to ignore what I had observed. There is also the fact that no-one at that stage could have foreseen the tremendous extent to which The Great Train Robbery and subsequent events were to grow. It is not in my nature, when the going gets tough, to turn round and say "I don't want to get involved."

I regret that my family suffered so much and that is the main reason why my recollections have remained private for so long.